UNDER
ASTRAL

Also in this series:

UNDERSTANDING ASTRAL PROJECTION

Exploration in a world beyond the body

by

Anthony Martin

Aquarian/Thorsons
An Imprint of HarperCollinsPublishers

The Aquarian Press
An Imprint of HarperCollins*Publishers*
77–85 Fulham Palace Road,
Hammersmith, London W6 8JB

First published by The Aquarian Press as
The Theory and Practice of Astral Projection 1980
This edition 1990
3   5   7   9   10   8   6   4   2

A catalogue record for this book
is available from the British Library

ISBN 0 85030 984 0

Printed in Great Britain by
HarperCollinsManufacturing Glasgow

CONTENTS

INTRODUCTION

St Paul, writing to the Church of Christ at Corinth, spoke of a man, known to the Apostle personally, who had been 'caught up to the third heaven', though whether he had enjoyed this mystical experience 'in the body' or 'out of the body' St Paul was unable to say.

St Paul's account (in 2 Corinthians 12:2) takes it for granted that such things were possible. This was no dream; no hallucination; the body could be left in a real sense. St Paul's terms are not always clear. Elsewhere he states, 'There is a natural body and there is a spiritual body', which may mean that there is a physical and an 'astral' body, or that there is an 'astral' body and a soul. One thing is clear, however: the experience St Paul described was for him an incontrovertibly real one.

It is, moreover, and always has been, a surprisingly common one. It seems to happen to people all the time, and not just to people of a religious or overtly 'sensitive' disposition. The feeling, to call it no more for the moment, of being separated from one's body can no longer be glibly dismissed as pure fantasy or imagination, and although in some cases the sensation is undoubtedly due to hallucination (while in others it is imperfectly remembered dreaming of an especially vivid kind), the evidence now seems overwhelmingly in favour of an altogether more momentous (and indeed logical) alternative: that it is possible to leave the physical body in a *second body* and still retain full consciousness and feeling; to be *yourself* while completely severed from the physical organism: to exist, as St Paul said, 'out of the body'.

The Pull of the Physical Body

It may be difficult, almost impossible, for many people to think of consciousness existing outside the physical body. We look after the body, pamper it, and worry constantly about its health and well-being. It is the inevitable focus of our waking life, so that a word like 'tragedy' has now lost its original association with a *spiritual* catastrophe and has become generally attached to *physical* disasters, principally bodily death or injury.

As a result of this concentration, it is all too easy for us to believe that the physical body, directed by the brain and by a myriad of miraculous chemical reactions, constitutes the sum of our being, even though this includes many things we know to be intangible and, in our present state of knowledge, incapable of being attributed to specific physical causes — memory for instance.

We can thus come to believe that everything we are is defined and bounded by this envelope of flesh, blood, bone and nerve endings. How simple it is for us to look in a mirror and feel convinced that the body we see reflected therein and the consciousness that directs and oversees its functions are somehow inseparably linked and that the one is inconceivable without the other. How simple, too, to take the next logical step and use this materialistic reduction as an argument against the survival of physical death. Is it really possible that intellect, reason, imagination, judgement, memory and perception, and all the other functions of consciousness, can exist in a pure form independently of the body?

Evidentially, the answer seems to be, yes: this is not only possible but habitual with some people, whilst for many others the severance of consciousness from the physical body is a temporary and rather startling accident.

The Religious Impulse

The unwillingness to believe in 'out-of-the-body experiences' is in large part a consequence of history. It is, comparatively speaking, a recent development. But the ancient and universal belief in the basic body and soul dichotomy seems to be vindicated by these experiences, which have reinstilled for many people a powerful sense of the spiritual aspect of life and of that elusive but crucial sense of meaning and significance that an all-pervasive materialism has now tended to overwhelm.

The sceptic might argue that the 'religious' impulse, by which I mean all assertions of non-physical realities, is in fact nothing more than a quirk of our psychological nature: we might be said to need these beliefs in the same way as the body needs certain vitamins and minerals in order to function efficiently. The brain (it could be said) compensates for the loss of belief by inventing or imagining experiences that seem to 'prove' the objective existence of a higher reality. It might, with some justice, be pointed out that the rise of materialism and technology in the nineteenth century, with the consequent diminution of the religious impulse, corresponded with an upsurge of interest in all aspects of the occult — fantasy in art, ghost stories, secret magical societies and spiritualism.

There are, doubtless, such compensatory mechanisms: the denial of a basic impulse must have its consequences, and the negation of spiritual aspirations — the breeding out, almost, of a belief in non-physical reality — may well produce curious and, as yet, unknown effects in the human psyche.

It is, after all, only a few hundred years since religion permeated the lives of almost every man and woman in Western Europe and produced, on the one side, the glory of the mediaeval cathedrals and, on the other, the degradations of the witch hunts. The submergence of religion has come about in a relatively short period of time (almost, one might say, overnight), and there may be some kind of collective trauma or delayed reaction as a result of this.

But in the last eighty years or so intensive investigations into psychic phenomena have uncovered so many testimonies to the reality of super-physical experiences that, combined with a historical study of similar phenomena, point irresistibly to the conclusion that out-of-the-body experiences, to take but one area of the so-called paranormal, are neither hallucinatory in every case nor are the compensations of a frustrated psychological need. The balanced verdict seems to be that they *exist*; they are *real*; they are *normal*.

The implications, of course, are very great indeed, because the probability of life after death is increased enormously if the objective reality of out-of-the-body experiences is established.

I have tried in this short survey to briefly sketch out the theoretical background to astral projection, and to the general concept of the occult anatomy of man, and to describe some of the many techniques that have been used successfully to project the astral body, thereby detaching consciousness from its shroud of flesh and blood.

The literature of astral projection and related subjects is enormous (the sources on which I have mainly drawn are indicated in the Notes and the Bibliography) and a book of this extent can make no claim for originality. I hope merely that this introductory guide will stimulate further investigation of a subject that is as fascinating as it is important and perhaps encourage that potent subconscious desire to go beyond the body.

CHAPTER ONE

THE THEORY OF ASTRAL PROJECTION

In 1886 the Society for Psychical Research published a pioneering census called *Phantasms of the Living*, which ran to over 1300 pages. The aim had been to collect and examine cases of spontaneous psychical phenomena and to subject them to detached scientific scrutiny. Many of the instances of what one of the authors, F.W.H. Myers, elsewhere called 'supernormal' happenings were explained by telepathy (which has now become almost respectable in scientific circles), i.e. the operation of one mind on another. Telepathy was even held responsible for so-called crisis apparitions, in which one person sees or hears another (who is usually known to the percipient) when the latter is on the point of or actually experiencing some acute personal crisis — often death itself.

The mind-to-mind theory is attractive and must account for many 'supernatural' happenings (though it is impressive enough as an indication of the mind's capability). But there remains a residue of experiences that cannot be explained satisfactorily by it. The literature of 'near-death' experiences, for instance, is now quite considerable.

George Ritchie

A typical case is that reported in the *Observer Magazine* of 8 April 1979. In December 1943 a twenty-year-old solder, George Ritchie, collapsed in front of an X-ray machine in an army hospital in Abilene, Texas, as a result of acute double pneumonia. He later 'died': there was no breath, no pulse, and no blood pressure. As his body was being prepared for the morgue a medical orderly thought he saw one of Ritchie's hands move. He immediately notified the doctor, who again pronounced the patient to be dead. In spite of this, the decision was taken to inject adrenalin directly into the heart which, to everyone's amazement, began to beat once more.

When George Ritchie recovered consciousness he had an incredible story to tell. As his body had lain on the hospital bed, with a sheet drawn over the face, Ritchie had, he claimed, been standing beside it observing everything. He claimed, too, that he had travelled over large areas of the United States; but it was the observation of what was happening to his own body that was most significant.

As he looked down at his body, the light
changed and brightened, a figure came into the
room and with it an altered experience of space
and time, so that Ritchie found himself
surrounded by a living panorama of all the
events of his life in complete clarity and detail.
The entrance of the figure of light ushered in a
still more far-reaching journey, from which he
returned to the pain of his lungs and high fever,
when the adrenalin jolted his heart back into
action.[1]

Dr Michael Sabom, Assistant Professor of
Cardiology at Atlanta, Georgia, has published
several specialist papers on near-death experiences
(NDEs) and some of his general conclusions are
worth quoting. Of the patients Dr Sabom
interviewed, 'At the time of unconsciousness, 29
patients experienced amnesia while 38 en-
countered a near-death experience (NDE): 18
experienced the passage of consciousness into a
foreign region or dimension (transcendence), 11
viewed their body and physical surroundings from
a detached position of height (autoscopy) and nine
both autoscopy and transcendence ...' Dr Sabom
concluded:

A definite decrease in death anxiety occurred in
most patients encountering NDE ... Although
adequate explanation of these phenomena is
not available, further investigation is needed
into the cause and implication of these
experiences.[2]

J.G. Bennett

A particularly vivid account of a near-death experience was given by J.G. Bennett in his autobiography *Witness*. During the First World War Bennett had been riding on a motor-cycle through Monchy-le-Preux just as the Germans were advancing. He remembered thinking to himself: 'If I get through Monchy, I shall be all right.' His next memory was of waking up, 'not inside — but outside my own body':

> I knew I was not dead. I could see nothing and hear nothing, and yet I perceived that my body was lying on a white bed. I gradually became aware that there were other men present, and somehow I was seeing what they saw and even feeling what they felt ... At that moment, it was perfectly clear to me that being dead is quite unlike being very ill or very weak or helpless. So far as I was concerned, there was no fear at all. And yet I have never been a brave man and I was certainly still afraid of heavy gun fire. I was cognizant of my complete indifference toward my own body.[3]

And yet, Bennett adds significantly, he was not totally disconnected from his body. 'He' accompanied 'it' to the operating theatre, after which he was observed by the medical staff to remain in a coma for six days. 'Yet I heard a voice saying: "Fine, please," and a woman's voice answer:

16

"There is only coarse left." Several days later, when I returned to consciousness and the stitches were taken out of my head, the nurse said: "I wonder why they used coarse hair." I said: "They had no fine left." She seemed surprised: "However do you know that? You were unconscious."'

Bennett also experienced an involuntary separation from his body some years later. After he had become associated with G.I. Gurdjieff it was the custom at meal times to have a ritual reading:

> Suddenly, without any warning, I found myself several feet away from my body. My voice was still speaking, but it was not 'my' voice any more, but a stranger's. I said to myself: 'How can he read? He can't possibly give the right intonation!' I could see the other people from quite a different perspective, and wondered if anyone else knew that an empty shell was reading. I wondered if Gurdjieff knew, and at the same moment the body's eyes looked up from the reading and saw him, and, without knowing how, I was back in my body again and the reading continued. The sense of separation from the body persisted for several hours, although I remained inside it.[4]

Science has not yet come up with a theory that can satisfactorily account for such experiences as these, which clearly cannot simply be dismissed as being invariably delusions. But theories do exist that, though not verifiable experimentally, do seem to make sense of an otherwise bewildering mass of personal testimonies, some of which involve quite involuntary dissociations from the physical body that are unrelated to trauma of any kind. The most impressive collections of cases of accidental severance are those by Dr Robert Crookall (see Bibliography), and I shall return to them later.

If we assume, then as a basic premise, that it may be possible for consciousness to remove itself from the physical body, how might this be done, and in what form does consciousness then exist?

Kingsland's Theory

William Kingsland, in his book *Rational Mysticism*, gave a clear account of the case for assuming that there exists within the physical body a super-physical double, for, as Kingsland maintained, it is contrary to all reason to think of consciousness operating without a body of some sort. Without a body, or a vehicle, there could indeed be no such thing as individual consciousness, for without a body, a limiting structure, there can be no individuality, only universality:

It is tolerably evident ... that if we are to believe in any conscious entities or beings whatsoever in the Universe, whether of a Cosmic or of a more limited nature, which have their existence independent of physical matter or physical bodies; or if we are to believe in any manner in our own conscious survival of bodily death,

> such individual survival, or such entities or
> beings, must have some substantial vehicle or
> body in or through which Life and
> Consciousness subsist, function or manifest
> objectively.[5]

Kingsland, in a valuable discussion of 'man's bodies', goes on to remark that such a vehicle cannot simply spring into existence on the death of the physical body: it must exist, fully formed, here and now; indeed, it may be seen as the energizing principle of the physical system, which is animated, not simply by physical sustenance, but by this vivifying body. Death, therefore, means not the disintegration of the physical system, but the final withdrawal of this vital 'etheric' body.

Materiality of the Astral Body

This is the basic theory of the double or, as we may now call it, the astral body. The word 'astral' comes from the Greek *aster*, meaning 'star', and for the Greeks the astral body denoted an envelope of 'star'-like material covering the soul (it was also called the *sidereal* body, from the Latin *sidus*, 'star').

It is generally thought that the astral body emits a luminous glow and is composed of some super-subtle matter vibrating at a very high rate. It is at once physical and ultra-physical. As far as it is composed of atomic matter, it has been thought possible to reveal some of the measurable characteristics of the astral body by scientific means. Dr Duncan McDougall of the Massachusetts General Hospital claimed to have measured a significant weight loss in patients at the moment of clinical death, due to the departure of the astral body. Dr Zaalberg Van Zelst in Holland has also claimed similar results.

Little or no work has been done in this area on people undergoing an out-of-the-body experience, though a note in the *Journal of the Society for Psychical Research* for March 1979 records that 'A long, careful and ingenious series of experiments on loss of body weight among sensitives was in fact carried out with a considerable number of subjects during the 1960s by John Cutten and other members of the Society following a suggestion by Arthur Koestler, who also provided the equipment.'[6] There were, however, no significant results.

The desire to establish the material qualities of the astral body has gone even further: some researchers have claimed that it can be seen at the moment of death leaving the body as a misty emanation. Mediums and sensitives of all kinds have reported seeing such emanations — sometimes a shapeless vapour, sometimes a recognizable human form. Eileen J. Garrett, the celebrated medium and clairvoyant, saw 'a curly, shadowy grey substance' rising from the body of her dead daughter. The following story is told by Archie Matson in his book *The Waiting World*:

The nurse tried to usher us out of the room. My father and sister left, but I stayed. The doctor then ordered me to leave. I had tossed my purse on a cot across the room, and started to get it when I had another strong feeling that would not be denied. I turned and looked at Mother. Her face was serene, and floating from her and above her toward the ceiling was a bright, golden, shapeless mist — heavier in some places than in others.

For a minute I held my breath — then, needing confirmation, I asked the doctor if he could see the same thing. He answered that he could, but that it was not unusual, and that it was 'gas escaping from the body'.[7]

The Soul

At the outset of any discussion of the astral body it is essential to distinguish it from the soul. Sir James Frazer, the author of *The Golden Bough*, wrote that 'Men in all stages of ignorance and knowledge commonly believe that when they die some part of them does not perish.' In this universal and continuing belief lies the essential distinction between the soul and the astral body.

The difference is quite fundamental: the astral body has a correlationship with the physical body and is an aspect of occult theory. The soul, on the other hand, is a religious concept and is, indissolubly, a fragment of eternity. The astral body is allied to materiality: it may perhaps even come to be scientifically weighed. And even though its constitution is largely unknown, theoretical and 'occult' (i.e. 'hidden'), it is nonetheless an aspect of physical being.

The soul, by contrast, is wholly non-physical. There are no correlations with materiality and we cannot begin to speculate on its constitution. It *is*, and therein is indicated its participation in a universal wholeness many would call God. The astral body is but a double, though of a finer nature, of the physical body: it is all individuality; but indwelling in it, the soul is a transcendent self-consciousness that at the same time partakes of an immutable completeness.

The soul, by all agreed definitions, is immortal and imperishable. The astral body may survive the death of the physical body for a time, but it too perishes in due course. It is worth noting also that, while religion is quite happy to concede that animals have astral bodies, it draws back from according them the privilege of possessing immortal souls.

Occult anatomy

Theosophy, the movement started by Colonel Olcott and Madame Blavatsky, developed a complex theory of man's occult anatomy. According to Theosophical teaching, there is not one subtle body, but many. A.E. Powell, for instance, wrote on the astral body, the mental body, the causal body and the etheric body. Broadly, the Theosophical view is that after death these various bodies are shed and consciousness is successively active in a number of 'layers', each with a corresponding form, each a recognizable personality, and each one ascending in a spiritual hierarchy.

Hereward Carrington gave a list of the names by which the double is known: the etheric body, the mental body, the spiritual body, the desire body, the radiant body, the resurrection body, the luminous body, the subtle body, the fluidic body, the shining body, the phantom body, and of course the astral body.[8] Distinctions abound, but for general purposes, the term astral body used to denote the subtle indwelling form is adequate

Disagreement on definitions and nomenclature is rife, though in a sense all the arguments are irrelevant. What is important is that some part of the totality of our being can detach itself from the physical body. What we choose to call this is of no ultimate consequence. What does seem clear is that the astral body, in Ralph Shirley's words, 'is as objective to consciousness as the physical body is on the physical plane'. In other words, the astral body, like the physical body, is a *vehicle*, within which resides the highest level of consciousness that we call the soul.

On the whole, the definitions of the occult anatomy used by Dr Robert Crookall are to be recommended. Each person, according to Dr Crookall's view, has a physical body and a soul. These are the two poles of his total bodily constitution. In addition there is a finer body — the astral body, associated with the astral planes. Between the physical body and the astral body is an atmosphere or aura, then an 'interspace', and then an astral atmosphere. The first, or physical, atmosphere is also called the vehicle of vitality and is analogous to the Scriptural 'breath of life' (Genesis 2:7, 6:17). It is semi-physical in nature and its function is to form a bridge between the physical body and the astral (or soul) body. The vehicle of vitality, as well as the astral body, can be projected, and astral projection can involve either or both:

> Some projections involve the Soul Body; others merely represent an extrusion of part of the vehicle of vitality; most are a combination of the two — the Soul Body goes out accompanied by a tincture of substance from the vehicle of vitality. In the latter circumstances the total non-physical body that is released is compound. In all cases it is a replica of the physical body: it is often called the *'double'*.[9]

Constitution of the Astral Body

Dr Hereward Carrington, one of the leading psychical investigators of this century, saw the astral body as being made up of 'psychomeres' or 'psychic centres'. In each cell in the body, he said, there is a nucleus of energy, an infinitely small focus of power, that vitalizes the physical matter in the cell:

Now, this centre of energy constitutes a sort of
psychic point or cell of its own, and as there
are millions of them in the body, corresponding
to the number of physical cells, it is obvious
that there are millions of vital cells which
conform exactly to the shape of the body, since
they correspond to its physical cells in life.[10]

Carrington also calculated the density of the astral
body (or 'etheric double') to be about one millionth
that of the physical body. Its weight, therefore, is
such that it would float easily through the physical
atmosphere if it were 'released', and indeed this
appears to be borne out by some of the testimonies
already quoted and by those who have experienced
spontaneous astral projection. A typical example is
cited by Dr Crookall:

'My son, then eight years of age, who had never
heard of anything of this sort, had gone to bed one
night and was lying reading. Suddenly he called
rather urgently for me. I found him sitting up, rather
scared. He said, "Such a funny thing has happened.
I was just lying reading when I felt I was rising into
the air. I seemed to go up near the ceiling. Then I
looked down and could see myself lying in bed. I
came slowly down. Then I called out."'[11]

The Silver Cord

The astral body is not always free floating: in many
cases it cannot go whither it will. It is connected to

25

the physical system by a cord, capable of stretching vast distances, but nevertheless an ever-present link with the material body. The existence of the cord is testified to by many astral travellers and appears in the earliest accounts. The classic reference is in the Bible, Ecclesiastes 12:6.

The cord is essentially an extension of the astral body and the connection with the physical body is such as to enable the latter's vital processes to continue; it could with propriety be called a life-line and has been compared on many occasions to the umbilical cord that supports the life processes of the unborn child. The severance of the astral cord, like the disconnection of the umbilical link, makes the re-entry of the double into the physical body impossible: this, as one astral projector said, is what death means.

From a consensus of the testimonies, the cord is luminous, like a stream of light. Its elastic property is often commented on — one traveller remembered 'the pull of the cord, as though it were made of stout elastic'. Its function is to transmit vitality from the astral to the physical body — a vitality greater and more essential than mere physical nourishment. Dr Crookall has suggested that the cord is in fact composite — that is, it is an extension of both the physical and the astral body. At death, the cord snaps, and part of it falls back into the physical body.

The point of attachment with the physical body appears to vary. Some testify that the astral and the physical bodies are attached by the head; others have seen the cord protruding from the back, the shoulders or from the navel. The cord can extend vast distances. At the beginning of separation it is some inches thick; when the two bodies are a number of feet apart, the cord becomes thinner; at greater distance it attenuates even further, to become an almost invisible thread. Some projectors, however, deny that the cord exists, seeing it as a panic-induced hallucination, a reassuring delusion based on the symbolical power of the umbilical cord. But most occultists reject this view.

During exteriorization the cord passes back vital energy to the inert physical body. When the two bodies are in normal coincidence the cord concentrates into a tiny knot, the location of which is usually said to be somewhere in the head or else between the shoulder blades. With the snapping of the cord — one of the basic fears surrounding astral projection — comes the death of the physical body. Perhaps the astral cord is at the root of a legend like the Greek Fates, the three sisters who spin the fates of men on a spindle, the most famous of whom is Atropos, who cuts the thread of life with her shears — a mythical representation, perhaps, of the severing of the silver cord.

The Experiences of Projection

The 'natural' manner of astral projection is when exteriorization is unforced by drugs, anaesthetic or conscious experimentation. In spontaneous projections the astral body usually leaves the physical via the head. Sylvan Muldoon, for instance, described a 'feeling as if consciousness were getting out of one's head'. The first sensations of projection vary, but some general features may be pointed out. Many projectors describe a feeling of rising; some, on the other hand, felt it as falling. Crookall's hypothesis was that 'with the former, consciousness was in the ascending "double" while with the latter it was in the body.'[12]

The Blackout

At the precise moment when the double is formed, a 'blackout' of consciousness is often experienced. This is often seen in terms of entering a dark tunnel. One theory is that, during the separation process, neither the body nor the double is available as an instrument of consciousness — hence there is a momentary break in consciousness, 'just as there is a brief break in transmission when we change gear in a car'.[13] Muldoon again: 'Just as the actual body leaves the physical, the consciousness grows dim for an instant, then comes back again.'

The Trail of Light

As the astral body moves, many say it leaves a trail of light behind it. The French psychic 'Yram' noticed a white luminous cloud trailing behind the double, whilst Muldoon remembered streaks of light, or 'scintillations', being thrown off by the astral body and extending backwards some two feet. Crookall ingeniously suggests that this tailback of neuric energy has often been observed in relation to the moving astral body and that it was this precise observation, and not pure fantasy, that gave rise to the idea that angels fly by means of 'wings'.

The Function of Sleep

Sleep is necessary not only for the renewal of physical vitality; its purpose is also to renew the vitality of the astral body. During sleep, the bonds which tie the astral to the physical body are relaxed, enabling the double to slip a little way outside of the physical body. Most people remain unaware of this discoincidence, but realizing that the astral body moves slightly out of coincidence every time you sleep is one of the basic steps in conscious projection.

Sleep is a disunion of the astral and the physical body, with the object of 'liberating' the astral double so that it may gather energy and vitality from astral sources, and is a form of astral projection that we all experience. As Hereward Carrington said: 'We shall never arrive at a satisfactory theory of sleep, doubtless, until we admit the presence of a vital force and the existence of an individual human spirit which withdraws more or less completely from the body during the hours of sleep and derives spiritual invigoration and nourishment during its sojourn in the spiritual world.'[14]

The astral body, then, is the ethereal counterpart of the physical body, which it resembles and with which it is normally in coincidence. Opinions on its actual composition vary, but it is generally thought to be formed of some subtle, or semi-fluidic, matter invisible (presumably as a result of a higher vibrational rate) to the physical eye.

The Nature of the Double

The astral double is a duplicate of the physical body in every detail — even down to clothes. It is the same with apparitions, where the body, as G.N.M. Tyrrell wrote, is 'just as clear and vivid in matters of detail, such as the colour and texture and clothing, as the material person'.[15]

Often, the similarity between the double and the physical body is so great and so exact that the subject may not realize he has left his physical body. This often happens after accidents when the subject simply is not aware that he has left his physical body lying injured on the ground but simply 'gets up' and walks away.

It should also be noted that not every experience involves the occupation of a second body: sometimes consciousness inhabits a wide range of spatial entities, from white clouds to imprecise shapes that nonetheless have a definite size and location in space.

It is often the case that the double is free from the defects of the physical body; that is to say, a sensory deficiency such as deafness or a defective sense of smell tends to be remedied in the astral body. Indeed, a feeling of well-being — unusually heightened in some cases — is usually the norm in the exteriorized state and many astral projectors feel somehow more 'real' in their astral bodies.

Occasionally a subject may experience bilocation — the feeling set up by there being, apparently, two centres of consciousness: one in the physical body and one in the astral double. 'My physical body was certainly conscious,' said one subject. 'It knew I was walking and seeing. What seemed to have escaped was whatever made the physical body me; i.e. whatever gave me personality or character.'[16]

Autoscopy and Autophany

There is a distinction to be borne in mind between autoscopy, the experience of *seeing oneself* (as in the case of George Ritchie, p.14) and autophany, *appearing to oneself* (i.e. the phenomenon associated in the past with doppelgängers: see p.43). Autoscopy assumes that consciousness is located beyond the physical body in such a way as to enable the subject to view the physical body from a distance and from a new focus of consciousness. In cases of autophany, the centre of consciousness remains in the physical body and is confronted by its double or astral replica.

The autoscopic experience nearly always accompanies astral projection, and it need not necessarily be associated with trauma. For instance, the double can 'escape' after fatigue:

> I was working as a waitress in a local restaurant and had just finished a 12 hour stint. I was terribly fatigued and was chagrined to find I had lost the last bus ... However I started walking as in those days I lived in Jericho, a fifteen minute walk at most. I remember feeling so fatigued that I wondered if I'd make it and resolved to myself that I'd 'got to keep going'. At this time I was where the Playhouse is today. The next I registered, was of hearing the sound of my heels very hollowly and I looked down and watched myself walk round the bend of Beaumont St into Walton St. I — the bit of me that counts — was up on a level with Worcester College Chapel. I saw myself very clearly — it was a summer evening and I was wearing a sleeveless shantung dress. I remember thinking, 'So that's how I look to other people.'[17]

Often the recognition that the physical body belongs to the subject leads to rapid interiorization. Most often, as here, subjects report looking *down* on their physical bodies.

Experimental Apparitions

Many apparitions are in fact the astral projections of living people rather than the ghosts of the dead. But there is another class of materialization — experimental apparitions. This is where an individual creates a phantom figure of himself at a distance by an effort of will or thought. There is, obviously, a close connection with conscious astral projection. Such apparitions may be induced, usually just before the subject falls asleep, by willing very strongly to appear before a certain person at a certain time. It can also be induced experimentally by means of hypnosis.

The distinction between experimental apparitions and deliberate astral projection is that the projection of a 'thought-form' does not necessarily imply the transfer of consciousness from the physical body to the projected form. In astral projection, this is always the case. An experimental apparition is merely a more or less solid image that has been made visible by an intense act of will. Astral projection, on the other hand, always involves a complete transfer of consciousnes, a severance of the essential 'I' from the physical body.

It is claimed that experimental apparitions can, in some cases, become endowed with self-consciousness, but this is by no means an automatic process, as in astral projection.

CHAPTER TWO

THE DOUBLE IN HISTORY

The materialistic position on the possibility that consciousness could survive beyond the physical destruction of the brain was stated succinctly by Dr C.D. Broad in 1925:

> The view that the mind is existentially dependent on the organism and on nothing else is compatible with all the normal facts, and is positively suggested by them, though they do not necessitate it. And it is the simplest possible view to take. The theory that the mind merely uses the body as an instrument is difficult to reconcile with the normal facts.[1]

This may be the simplest view to take, and on the face of things it seems unanswerable. But the opposite view is exactly what hundreds of personal testimonies and centuries of occult and mystical experience have definitely (one might say defiantly) asserted: that consciousness does not reside in the physical structure of the brain, but that within the physical body is another entity, which is the actual vehicle of consciousness.

The French psychical investigator Hector Durville (see p.72) posed a fundamental question: are sensations perceived by the *visible* body, or by the *invisible* body which interpenetrates and animates it? The materialist would answer that there is no question about it; that the physical brain is the sole location of consciousness. But Durville claimed that the results of his experiments proved that the visible, material body was indeed merely an instrument which the subtle, invisible body used as a means of self-expression. His method was to hypnotize both the physical body and the exteriorized double. His subjects invariably claimed that real individuality resided in the projected phantom, not in the physical body. One of them stated: 'The body which you touch is nothing at all. It is merely a shell or covering of the other. All my individuality is in the luminous phantom. It is that which thinks, which has consciousness and which acts. It transmits to its physical counterpart what I am saying to you.'[2]

Oriental Theories of the Astral Body

Ancient Chinese teachings reveal a well-developed theory of the astral or vital body. According to Taoist texts, the radiant energy ('the Light') of the universe was concentrated in the physical body in the form of a spiritual essence. This was usually inert but by special exercises and meditative techniques it could be activated and made to exteriorize in a spatial form. Rhythmic breathing, meditation, and techniques such as concentrating on the end of the nose were used to bring this about. The vital body, thus energized, leaves the physical body via the head, while the physical body remains in a trance state.

There is an illustration in Richard Wilhelm's translation of *The Secret of the Golden Flower* that shows the third stage of meditation, 'Separation of the spirit-body for independent existence', in which a small figure is seated on a cloud that hovers above a meditator, to whose head it is attached by a cloudy cord.

Hindu philosophy postulated an occult anatomy consisting of the physical body, the subtle body and the causal body or soul. The mediating, subtle body, houses such things as sensory perception and the mental mechanism whereby we are able to recognize ourselves as individuals.

Tibetan occult teachings naturally have much to say on the subject. According to these, everything — living and non-living — has a double, a shadow reality that exists in a dimension that interpenetrates our own. The human double thus inhabits two worlds at once. The double is normally invisible, but it can be seen by those trained in second sight. It moves out of coincidence with the physical body during sleep and during certain types of meditation. When the physical body dies, the double eventually disintegrates.

The ancient yoga texts speak of the eight *siddhis* or supernormal powers that can be achieved through the practice of a particular type of yoga. One of these is known as 'flying in the sky', which seems to refer to what we would now call astral travel.

The Theory of the Astral Double in the West

Strands of a belief in the astral or starry body began to be gathered together in classical Greece and we can see the theory of the starry envelope of the soul taking shape in the writings of Plato, Aristotle and the third-century Platonist, Porphyry.

In Dante's *Purgatorio*, written in the fourteenth century, is a reference to the soul beaming round its own creative power, 'like to its living form in shape and size ... the circumambient air adopts the shape the soul imposes on it.'

In the Renaissance, the revival of interest in classical philosophy, especially the more esoteric and mystical aspects, led to renewed speculation on the function and nature of the astral double. The Neoplatonist Jean Fernel (1497-1558), for instance, referred to the Greek teachings on the subject and to the assumption that two such dissimilar natures as the body and the soul could not exist in harmonious association without the help of some mediating agent. The soul, according to Neoplatonic theory, was enveloped in a shining garment, a vehicle that interposed between the two natures of man — the physical body and the soul. They also taught that this second body or garment was made from stellar material, and hence was particularly susceptible to astrological influences.

Paracelsus formulated a sevenfold constitution of man, one element of which was the astral body, whilst the abstruse speculations of the alchemical philosophers spoke, in characteristically guarded symbolism, of an entity we can perhaps recognize as the astral body.

Exteriorization

The material and the astral bodies are, under normal conditions, locked together in a single unit, the one interpenetrated by the other. Discoincidence only occurs during unconsciousness or when the physical body is asleep. Conscious projection, therefore, is achieved by simulating these conditions.

Mystics throughout history have recognized the reality of the exteriorized astral double, though it is usually carefully distinguished from the soul. Yoga is a means whereby discoincidence can be achieved and, at its highest levels, yoga can lead to the disassociation of consciousness entirely from the physical body and even entry into other planes of reality. Neoplatonism, as we have seen, laid stress on the presence of the astral within the material body and they emphasized the slender link between the two. According to Neoplatonic theory, the astral body could break free from its physical moorings during sleep or in a trance state, and one of their maxims was that the night-time of the body is the day-time of the soul. Plotinus himself recorded that he had been many times 'lifted out of the body' to become 'external' to all things.

Some people, of course, have always been more prone to involuntary astral travel than others. It seems to be a concomitant of the mystical temperament and is also associated with artistic creativity. Certain physical types are also more likely to undergo spontaneous discoincidence — those, for instance, of a weak or nervous constitution allied with a lively, sensitive mentality. The tales of witches flying to sabbaths may also have their origin in actual cases of astral travel.

One estimate is that about one in every hundred people experience some form of astral projection at least once in their lives. Indeed, though the mystic or the highly-strung artist may on the whole be likely to experience multiple projections, out-of-the-body journeys happen to a great many ordinary and 'unlikely' people — as shown by the statistical researches of Professor Hornell Hart at Duke University, North Carolina, and Celia Green at Oxford, as well as by the numerous case histories collected by Dr Crookall.

Dreams or Reality?

One important question needs to be faced at the

outset: are out-of-the-body experiences dreams or reality? Sceptics of course argue that they are dreams, pure and simple. But the testimonies of astral travellers impress above all by their sense of *reality*: it is, quite literally, an *experience* that is being described, not an hallucination. In dreams, the personality is dissolved, as it were, and the critical faculties lie dormant. We observe in a strange, detached and almost helpless way. But during astral travel, the personality is fully engaged, and consciousness, with all its faculties, operates with normal, and usually above normal efficiency.

Duality in Ancient Beliefs

Since the dawn of his life on earth man has been incurably convinced that this physical body encloses something altogether more permanent. That 'something' is necessarily non-physical and indestructible, and although for most of the time it coexists with the body and conforms in every way to it, it is capable under certain conditions of becoming detached from it and can assume a completely independent existence.

There have been many developments from this basic idea. Most primitive societies believe in the survival of a permanent spiritual entity existing after the physical body has died. In some cases the spirit is part of a huge communal reservoir or tribal substance: on the death of one member the soul merges with the tribal substance and provides the material for new-born members. In others, the soul is thought to lodge in a variety of objects — a tree, a rock, or an animal.

Egyptian Theory

In ancient Egypt this primal impulse to theorize about an essential immateriality and immortality within the physical body became highly developed. The Egyptians' belief in a future life was fundamental to their culture: it interpenetrated everything they did. They could not think that the body's dissolution defined the period of their existence. 'They knew quite well,' wrote E.A. Wallis Budge, 'that the physical body of a man could not live for ever, for they had daily proof before their eyes that the dead *did* "see corruption" ... Yet their faith in the future life never wavered, and they came to the conclusion that there must be in the corruptible body a something which could be separated from it and would live after the death of its body.'[3]

The tomb thus became the 'everlasting house' within which resided the *ka* or genius of the deceased body. As long as the mummy of the perishable body remained there, so long did the *ka* remain. It might go in and out of the tomb, and even refresh itself with food and drink, but it never failed to return to the mummy. The *ba* or soul, and the *chu*, or intelligence, on the other hand, did not live in the tomb.

The hieroglyphic texts speak of the *ka* as a duplicate of the body, a 'fluidic spirit'. The Egyptians seem to have thought of it as a less dense copy of the physical body, a replica in every detail. Its attachment to the physical body even after death explains why ancient Egypt placed so great an emphasis on embalming, which was an attempt to save the body from decomposition.

The *ka*, then, was not analogous to what we generally mean by the soul: its existence had a theoretical limitation. It appears to have denoted some kind of vital force that was essential in life and attached to the body in death as long as the body lasted. In this we see the basic characteristics of what later came to be called the astral body.

The Double

Behind all the modern theories of the constitution and metaphysics of the human double lie centuries of belief in the ability of the soul, the immortal part of man, to take visible form.

We now differentiate between the astral body and the soul and, as we have seen, the occult anatomy of man has been divided into even more component parts. But at the root of it all is the concept of the double.

We find the notion of the double in the folklore of all cultures. Confrontation with the double was considered to be an extremely bad omen: the Greeks, for instance, avoided looking at their reflections in water. The shadow, too, was seen as the dark side of the self, perpetually (though not always visible) in attendance.

The psychological implications of having a double, often of an evil nature, inhabiting the physical body is, of course, a potent literary theme: Stevenson's *Dr Jekyll and Mr Hyde* and Oscar Wilde's *The Portrait of Dorian Gray* are two famous examples. But there are numerous real life incidents that involve the confrontation with the double, usually with dire consequences.

Autophany: The Doppelgänger Phenomena

D.G. Rossetti's well-known painting 'How They Met Themselves' shows the doppelgänger legend at its most romantic. Meeting oneself is a comparatively rare phenomena, but one that has involved a number of famous people.

John Aubrey, the seventeenth-century antiquary and gossip, recorded how Lady Diana Rich was walking in the grounds of Holland House when she saw a vision of herself as clearly as a reflection in a mirror. A month later she was dead.

Queen Elizabeth I also saw her own wraith shortly before her death, as did Catherine the Great. Shelley saw his double pointing towards the sea, indicating, as it turned out, that the poet was to meet death by drowning.

Meeting oneself is not always followed by death.

Goethe recounted meeting his doppelgänger in his book *Aus Meinem Leben*:

> I was riding on the footpath towards
> Drusenheim, and there one of the strangest
> presentiments occurred to me. I saw myself
> coming to meet myself on the same road on
> horseback, but in clothes such as I had never
> worn. They were of light grey mixed with gold.
> As soon as I had aroused myself from this
> daydream the vision disappeared. Strange,
> however, it is that eight years later I found
> myself on the identical spot, intending to visit
> Frederika once more, and in the same clothes
> which I had seen in my vision, and which I
> now wore, not from choice, but by accident.

There is also what seems to be a reference to the double in the Bible. When St Peter was released from prison by the angel, he went and knocked at the door of a place where many of his friends were gathered. They could not believe that it was actually him and told the girl who opened the door, 'It is his angel.' Catherine Crowe, in *The Night-Side of Nature*, asked what they meant by this.

> The expression is not *an* angel, but *his* angel.
> Now, it is not a little remarkable, that in the
> East, to this day, a double, or doppelgänger, is
> called a man's angel, or messenger. As we can
> not suppose that this term was used otherwise
> than seriously by the disciples that were
> gathered together in Mark's house ... we are

> entitled to believe they alluded to some
> recognized phenomenon. They knew, either
> that the likeness of a man — his spiritual self —
> sometimes appeared where bodily he was not;
> and that this *imago* or *idolon* was capable of
> exerting a mechanical force, or else that other
> spirits sometimes assumed a mortal form ...[4]

Mrs Crowe, in her remarkable book, then goes on to record instances of the classic doppelgänger situation, which emphasize that the experience of meeting oneself, unlike that of Goethe's, usually forbodes disaster. Two of her cases may be briefly mentioned. The first concerned a jeweller from Ludwigsburg called Ratzel. One evening, in perfect health, he turned a corner and met his own form, face to face. He was so close that he looked into the very eyes of the simulacrum. He was terror-struck, but the doppelgänger vanished. He told several people of his experience and impressed his hearers with his sincerity. Shortly afterwards, he passed through a forest and met a band of wood-cutters who asked Ratzel to lend a hand to the ropes with which they were pulling down an oak tree. He did so and was killed by its fall.

The second is the case of Becker, a professor of mathematics at Rostock. He had been arguing a theological point with some friends and went to his library to fetch a book to which he wished to refer. On entering the library he saw himself sitting in his usual chair reading. He approached the figure from behind, looked over its shoulder, and saw that it was reading the Bible. The fingers of the right hand of the doppelgänger pointed to the passage: 'Make ready thy house, for thou must die.' Professor Becker, having told his friends what had happened, died the following evening.

Saintly Doubles

The doubles of saints are usually said to be capable of loosing themselves with ease and often have the ability to appear with such distinctness and solidity as to convince witnesses that they are looking at the physical form. There are two celebrated examples of this happening.

The first concerns St Anthony of Padua. One Holy Thursday he was taking a service in the Church of St Pierre du Queyrrix at Limoges when he suddenly recalled that he had engaged to be present at a service at the other end of the town. He drew his hood over his head and knelt down. It was later reported that he had appeared before the congregation of monks at the other service, read the lesson and the appointed office, and then vanished.

The second case is that of St Alphonsus Liguori, who died in 1787. He suffered from chronic ill health and in the autumn of 1774 he had fallen into a trance and remained in his cell in the monastery of Arezzo for five days, immobile. At the end of this period he regained consciousness and announced that he had been at the death-bed of Pope Clement XIV, some four days' journey away. The details of his statement were subsequently confirmed and he was actually seen at the Pope's bedside.

Goethe's Friend

Goethe (whose family, said Mrs Crowe, were ghostseers) is the source of another story of meeting a double that had every appearance of reality — again with no serious consequences.

One summer evening Goethe was walking home with a friend when he saw an old acquaintance called Friedrich coming towards him. Friedrich, to Goethe's amazement, was dressed in a dressing-gown, nightcap and slippers. His friend saw nothing of Friedrich. On arriving home, Goethe actually found Friedrich. He had been soaked in a rainstorm and had changed his wet clothes at Goethe's house. He was dressed exactly as Goethe had seen him on the road and he heard from Friedrich that he had dozed off and dreamt that he had gone to meet his friend.

Sir Carne Rasch

This is another well-known case, involving three Members of Parliament. Sir Carne Rasch was ill in bed but was seen distinctly in the House of Commons on the same occasion by two friends of his. One of them, Sir Arthur Hayter, claimed that he had seen Rasch that morning looking extremely pale and that he was sitting some distance away from his usual place. The other witness, Sir Gilbert Parker, nodded at Rasch and asked him how he was, only to be met with a silent glare from Rasch, who then vanished.

CHAPTER THREE

THE PRACTICE OF ASTRAL PROJECTION

Like all psychic activities, astral projection can be dangerous. Dissociation can be a hazardous business and it is well for all those intending to experiment in this area to take the warnings of those who have gone before them very seriously indeed. To become separated from the body during an illness or, like J.G. Bennett, after an accident, usually has no lasting ill effects; but to wilfully enforce exteriorization is quite another matter. It is even possible, as some have claimed, for the astral body to become damaged — a condition indicated by a corresponding change in the aura.

The nervous system can suffer permanent damage by a too violent return to the physical body; the astral body can also become misaligned. The physical body itself can be affected with symptoms of nausea, dizziness or even paralysis. But the dangers to the spiritual nature are of more moment. As Benjamin Walker has written:

In extreme cases the hinder side of things, normally concealed in the unconscious, might turn about and merge with the events of everyday life. An even more serious possibility is also to be envisaged. The astral body is intimately connected, no one knows by what mysterious corridors, to the inner recesses of the self, perhaps even the soul, and incautious experiments with astral projection would involve tampering with the delicate balance of this relationship, resulting in a progressive disintegration of the psyche.[1]

Catalepsy is another very real danger when consciousness is transferred from the physical to the etheric body, and with that comes the added possibility of premature burial through being certified dead when in fact consciousness remains in the physical body.

The inner planes themselves are full of terrors and traps for the unwary. There are elemental forces that even the experienced dread and avoid. 'Those who enter into relations with the powers of the astral and elemental,' wrote Anna Kingsford, 'without having made sure of their hold on the celestial, render themselves accessible to the infernal.'[2]

The Experience of Astral Projection

With the dangers fully and permanently in mind,

then, what can the novice experimenter expect to experience when the techniques of astral projection have been mastered?

The classic, and still thrilling, account is by Sylvan Muldoon in *The Projection of the Astral Body*. Muldoon, from a very early age, had a singular capacity for projecting his astral body at will. He was always a rather weak and sickly person, which may well have had a significant effect on his ability to exteriorize. His first experience occurred when he was twelve years old. He was taken by his mother to the camp of the Mississippi Valley Spiritualist Association at Clinton, Iowa. On the night of their arrival Muldoon retired to bed at about 10.30 p.m., sleeping for some three hours. He then realized that he was slowly waking up but could neither drift back into sleep nor awake into normal consciousness.

He was, he said, in 'a powerless, silent, dark and feelingless condition'. In this state of 'astral catalepsy' he suddenly felt himself to be floating. At the same time, his entire body began vibrating at a great rate and there was a tremendous pressure on the back of his head.

He then realized that he was indeed floating a few feet above his bed. He moved, involuntarily it seemed, from a horizontal to an upright position on the floor. Finding he could now move, he turned and saw for the first time that his physical body was still lying on the bed. There were now two identical bodies, joined by an elastic-like cable, one end of which was fastened to the medulla oblongata area of the astral body, the other fixed between the eyes of its physical counterpart.

He was able to walk about and pass through apparently solid matter such as doors. Eventually he felt resistance in the cable increase; he lost all control and suddenly found himself once again in a horizontal position above the bed:

> It was the reverse procedure to that which I had experienced while rising from the bed. Slowly the phantom lowered, vibrating again as it did so, then it dropped suddenly, coinciding with the physical counterpart once more. At this moment of coincidence, every muscle in the physical jerked and a penetrating pain, as if I had been split open from head to foot, shot through me. I was physically alive again, filled with awe, as amazed as fearful, and I had been conscious throughout the entire occurrence.

Desire

The single most important factor in deliberate astral projection is the *desire to leave the physical body*. Without this conscious determination nothing will be accomplished. Once the desire has been conceived it usually slips below the threshold of consciousness, remaining, however, as an extremely potent trigger. Indeed, desire of any kind, especially if it is suppressed, can be used to fuel the projection processes. Muldoon, for instance, exploited the power of suppressed desire by drinking salt water just before going to sleep. His physical body was inert and incapacitated; but his astral body released itself because of the desire to drink water.

Once astral projection has been achieved, the desire to repeat the experience increases and this compounding of the will to project makes subsequent exteriorizations easier.

Spontaneous projection, as we have seen, is one thing. The experience is a totality, and the subject observes the process with a kind of puzzled objectivity. But in deliberate projection the various stages of disassociation must be clearly understood and practised. There are three main stages.

The First Stage

The first stage is when the astral body is placed just slightly out of alignment with the physical body. This, as stated, before, is what happens in sleep and the nonphysical benefits of a really good night's sleep — for example, renewed mental vigour and intellectual energy — derive from the astral body's disassociation with the physical body and its brief but essential sojourn on the astral planes. The ability *to become aware that the physical body is asleep* is the first stage of astral projection. This means nothing less than that full consciousness is existing independently of the sleeping body, and, most importantly, outside it.

This experience is more common than one might at first suppose and most people are not aware that it is a form of astral projection. Extreme tiredness, for instance, can often bring about the release of the astral body. The physical body is exhausted, and yet sleep does not come. The mind continues to race, images crowd upon the brain, and recent experiences, often those that have brought about the physical exhaustion, are relived. Sometimes these 'action replays' can be very vivid indeed and in these cases consciousness has moved beyond the physical body: you become unaware of your physical tiredness and the experience you are reliving in a kind of waking dream takes over as the astral body, now the sole vehicle of consciousness, slips a little way beyond the physical shell.

The Second Stage

The kind of dissociation described above is something many of us have experienced. The next stage is less common for most people but is very well documented. This involves the actual removal of the astral body from the physical sheath for a distance of some feet or even yards. It is often triggered off by an accident to the physical body that involves trauma. J.G. Bennett's experience in France (see p.16) is a good example, and the situation where a patient finds himself looking down on his physical body surrounded by a medical team (as in the case of George Ritchie, p.14) is also common in the literature of the subject.

The Third Stage

This is when the astral body is moved to a considerable distance away from the physical body: some travellers claim to have covered vast distances in the astral body. Most often, projections across great distances are motivated by a strong desire to be at a particular place or to be with a particular person. Here the desire factor is clearly in evidence: desire becomes creative — a source of energy that can propel the astral body to its goal.

The Creative Imagination

To project deliberately requires the utilization of desire, as previously mentioned, as well as the ability to visualize strongly and clearly. It is, in effect, a form of self-hypnosis. The images you can use to suggest projection are various: escape from one physical environment to another is a good example. You might imagine being anchored in some way to the sea bed and needing desperately to force your way to the surface. Perhaps you might picture yourself on one side of a wall in a desert area and trying to vault or climb the wall to gain access to a lush green landscape on the other side. Again, the desire factor is of supreme importance.

Preliminary Exercises for Releasing the Double

The best time to try projecting in this way is when the physical body is tired and capable of relaxing quickly and when the mind is relatively alert — the desire to project, if strong enough, will often keep the mind active even when you are physically exhausted.

Lie flat: the floor rather than a bed is the best place. The secret is to relax the body while at the same time emptying the mind of everything except the desire to move beyond the physical body. The physical environment needs to be quiet and peaceful. Semi-darkness is especially conducive to projection. Some projectionists maintain that the period just before midnight to about three hours after is the best time, as this is when the body is normally in deep sleep.

The pressures of everyday life must be completely ignored: your muscles as well as your mind must be relaxed and all tension must be overcome. You must not even be anxious to succeed in projecting, as anxiety of any kind is a barrier to successful astral projection. If exteriorization fails to occur, the failure must simply be accepted and another attempt made at a later date. And while the desire to project is of paramount importance, it must not be pursued too intensely so as to become an obsession.

Desire can be harnessed most effectively in short bursts, concentrating all the mental energies on the one specific objective of projection. The will to appear to another person is the cause of many so-called apparitions, a famous example of which involved the Swedish playwright August Strindberg. Strindberg was in Paris in 1895 and was in a state of intense mental turmoil after the breakdown of his second marriage. In this condition he felt an overwhelming longing to be with his family once again and he suddenly found himself back at home and clearly saw his mother-in-law sitting at the piano. She saw him just as clearly and indeed asked him later in a letter if he were ill.

Visualization

This is the second great key to successful astral projection. Visualization has been at the heart of all occult exercises and is indeed the principal gateway to the inner planes. The creative imagination, for that is what visualization really is, of course has a long and distinguished pedigree, being the living heart of certain kinds of poetry and other forms of artistic creativity.

Visualization is not easy: it is something we have grown away from, having relied for so long on retrieval systems — from books to computers. We no longer have to rely so heavily on memory and the recall of mental images is no longer an important factor in the survival game.

Try some simple experiments: look at the cover of a book; close the eyes and try to picture to yourself an exact mental replica of it, correct in every detail. You will find that it is far from easy to conjure up an exact mental image of the cover; but if you persevere, perhaps for a hundred times, you will begin to find that the image takes on increasing clarity and exactness, until at last you can see mentally as clearly and as precisely as you can with your physical sight. When you can do this, you have mastered a basic technique in astral projection and one that you can put to immediate use.

Visualization Exercises

In the first stages of conscious astral projection, visualization is all-important. Try first of all to 'loosen' the astral body by the use of this new power of creative visualization. Lie back, on the bed or on the floor, and visualize your astral body rising a little way above your physical body; *really* visualize this happening, do not merely think about it.

Observe what is happening in minute detail, including your surroundings. While doing so, blot out the sensation of the bed or the floor beneath your back; erase the very thought from your consciousness that you are being supported by matter.

Concentrate solely and intently on your astral body as it gently looses itself from its physical moorings and hovers in the air.

You may try this exercise time and again without anything happening. If you continue to remain firmly locked in the physical body you must intensify your visualization exercises: some people's astral body is much more tightly enmeshed in the physical than others and it requires tremendous concentration and application to release it.

Transferring Consciousness

When you try once more to project you must try to make the jump from imagination to experience: as you visualize the astral body floating above the physical body you must strive to transfer your consciousness to the astral, and this must be done with such completeness that you can watch your physical body lying inert on the bed or on the floor. You must truly and actually observe *from* the astral body.

Be content with small successes. Every step you take is a difficult one and requires complete dedication if you are not a person who slips easily into the astral. Try to imagine your astral body moving, turning, rotating; transfer all your energy to the astral body, leaving the physical body what it in fact is — a lifeless shell.

Visualizing With the Eyes Open

The exercises so far mentioned are done with the eyes shut. The next stage involves visualizing with the eyes open. This is even more difficult, but becomes easier with practice and when the eyes-closed techniques have been mastered. Lie down, with the eyes open, and begin to loosen the astral body by visualizing its dissociation from the physical body. Begin with the feet and imagine the luminous double disentangling itself and forming phantom feet; work your way up the body, slowly and carefully, until you can see a glowing double of yourself distinctly.

Many astral projectors maintain that the course of the released double is often spirally from the head, and this course can be visualized in order to induce projection. As Crookall says, 'if one *imagines* the astral body spiralling out, it definitely tends to do so.'[3]

Concentration

Other methods that can be tried, supplementing the above visualization exercises, include staring fixedly at a single object some distance away. This can quickly lead to dissociation, as the eyes lose their power to focus properly and the unconscious mind swings into action.

A candle placed at the far end of a darkened room is a good focusing point. When you feel your normal consciousness becoming suspended, visualize your astral body moving out and away from your physical body and towards the object of your gaze — the candle.

Another method, adopted by the practitioners of Eckankar, involves the use of a coloured disc placed between the eyebrows, at which you stare without blinking.

Mantras

Other ancient techniques rely on the chanting of mantras or magical syllables; such monotonous chanting over long periods induces a trance state in which the astral body is capable of being loosed. This technique was used from boyhood by Lord Tennyson to bring about dissociated states: 'This has come upon me through repeating my own name to myself silently, till all at once, as it were out of the intensity of the consciousness of individuality, individuality itself seemed to dissolve and fade away into boundless being, and this is not a confused state, but the clearest of the clearest.'

Beads or rosaries, fingered while some mystical or cryptic verse or sound is chanted, is yet another ancient device for transcending the physical plane and is often carried out with specific breathing exercises (see p.64) that decrease the amount of carbon dioxide in the blood — though deep breathing is a dangerous method for the novice and should only be attempted with full knowledge, and even then with care.

The Opening Door Technique

But always we return to visualization. A well-known occult technique was devised by Aleister Crowley. The projector has to imagine a closed door in a blank wall. Inscribed on the door is a glyph that has previously been the subject of the projector's meditation. It is then necessary to visualize the door slowly opening and then to see yourself pass through it. With practice (and luck) exteriorization will occur, as it did with Kenneth Grant, who tried Crowley's technique and reported that he suddenly found himself 'bereft of my body; a sensation of extreme lightness and freedom characterized my movements'.[4]

Use of Specific Images

It has been found that certain images can facilitate the release of the astral double. Such images will operate on every individual in a different way, but it is worth while concentrating on a few to see if there is any perceptible slackening of the bond between the physical and astral bodies.

Try imagining ripples or flashes of light (again, *really* see them); imagine yourself as a point in space, floating freely, or as a fragment of cloud, or as steam (many projectors have found this analogy with steam to be an effective means of release).

Movement, as previously mentioned, can be a useful method, such as images of flying or twirling in space. The image of a cone can be used, since this involves the notion of contracting to a point or expanding from a primary focus. You can imagine passing through a cone to a luminous world beyond; the image of a whirlpool is often associated with the cone, for similar reasons. Whirling, we remember, is a principal feature of the dances by which dervishes put themselves into a trance.

The idea behind concentrating on such images is that imagination actually creates the conditions in the astral world. What we call imagining is nothing but the exercise of the astral senses: 'Whereas in this world, if we imagine ourselves as going to a certain city, our thought is the only result, in the astral world we should go there, at least if we wished.'[5]

In other words, thought is a creative act in the astral world, and if we imagine the astral body whirling towards a narrow point of release or climbing out of the physical body, this will inevitably encourage these actions to take place: the thought is enough to set the astral body in motion, although we may not be aware in the physical body that this is so. Muldoon spoke of the passive and the active will, the former being much the stronger and the will that we have at our disposal when we wake up at the dead of night; and he says categorically, 'Perhaps you will say, "What are you trying to make us believe? That one can project by merely imagining that he can?" In one sense this is truer than you might think ... The imaginative will *can* cause the projection of the astral body.'[6]

The tunnel image is perhaps the most basic and effective means of stimulating the imaginative will, simply because it appears to correspond with the actual sensations of projection. It may be compared with the experience of many patients under anaesthetic who describe the sensation of 'going under' as like passing down a long dark tunnel.

Breathing

The manipulation of breathing, as previously mentioned, has long been known to provide an entry to trance states and to encourage release of the astral body. Simply holding the breath will produce a slight loosening of the astral body; as Swedenborg wrote, 'Retaining or holding back the breath is equivalent to having intercourse with the soul, drawing it with the body.' The higher levels of yoga, of course, lay great stress on the psychic effects of breath control.

'Counting the Steps'

The Shinto magicians of Japan perfected a method of astral travel known as 'Counting the Steps', and an adaptation of this technique is amongst the easiest and most effective for the novice astral traveller.

It is based on an accurate visualization of a specific journey, usually to visit a loved one. The magicians decided on a given number of paces that would complete the journey — no matter how far, in everyday terms, the distance was.

Imagining himself leaving his house, the magician sees himself taking the required number of paces and then arriving at the door of the house he wishes to visit. He then has to knock at the door and be admitted by the person he desires to see.

When he has delivered his message he must take the same number of steps back to his own house. Enormous concentration and precise, vivid visualization are required for this technique.

The adaptation is as follows. First of all, decide on a route to follow in your own home — say, from bedroom to kitchen. You must then acquaint yourself with the minute physical particulars of that route; every single detail must be embedded in your mind. Go over it time and time again; draw out the route on a piece of paper and fill in the main characteristics. Do anything to familiarize yourself with the route.

Then select about six points along the route — an electric power point, perhaps, or a radiator or a picture on the wall.

You must then sit before each selected point and look steadily at it for about five minutes. Return to the same spot the next day and concentrate on the spot for about ten minutes.

Repeat this exercise for as long as is necessary to fix that spot *exactly* in your memory, and then go on to the other points you have selected along the route.

When you feel you have every single detail of the route and the points along it indelibly imprinted on your memory you are ready to attempt a journey along the route in your astral body.

Lie in bed and relax. As the body sinks into inertia visualize yourself rising from the bed in your astral body. To begin with, you will be observing the imaginary form of your double from your physical body; but if you have prepared yourself carefully and have become used to vivid visualization, a state of dual consciousness should take over, followed by a transfer of consciousness to the astral form itself.

Try to 'hold' yourself in the astral image; see *from* the astral body and go slowly over the route you should have come to know so well. Linger at every chosen point and take stock of every memorized detail.

Eventually you will reach the end of the route. You can then return immediately to your physical body, or you can go back along the route. On returning, it may seem like a vivid dream; but after several attempts you will begin to realize that you have been actually travelling in your astral body.

As you become more adept you can simply project through the accumulation of desire, creating an intense vision of a place you wish to be in.

Sustained literary composition, as I have found, can also induce a preliminary state of dissociation: when the fever hits the writer his thoughts tumble out quicker than he can write, and in this state of extreme creative excitement the astral threshold comes closer, indicated by a feeling of light-headedness as the eyes become unfocused and, once again, the unconscious mind wells up, blotting out the petty temporal preoccupations of everyday consciousness.

Oliver Fox

The experiences of Oliver Fox, reported in the

Occult Review in 1920, are among the most famous in the whole literature of astral projection. The articles in which Fox recounted his astral projections were called 'The Pineal Doorway' and 'Beyond the Pineal Door', and in them are a number of fascinating details.

Fox began by setting down the two alternative explanations for experiences such as his: 1) that they were vivid dreams, 2) that they were actual projections of an inner body. He himself made no attempt to prove the theory of an astral body; he merely laid his experiences before the reader.

The main feature of Oliver Fox's astral projections was that they emanated from dream control. His technique, now famous was *to observe some incongruity or anachronism in a dream*; in other words, one acquires the knowledge that one is dreaming. It is worth quoting Fox's discovery of the dream key:

Eighteen years ago, when I was a student at a technical college, a dream impelled me to start my research. I dreamed simply that I was standing outside my home. Looking down, I discovered that the paving stones had mysteriously changed their position — the long sides were now parallel to the curb instead of perpendicular to it. Then the solution flashed upon me: Though that glorious summer morning seemed as real as could be, I was *dreaming!* Instantly the vividness of life increased a hundredfold. Never had sea and sky and trees shone with such glamorous beauty; even the commonplace houses seemed alive and mystically beautiful. Never had I felt so absolutely well, so clear-brained, so divinely powerful. Verily the world had become my oyster. The sensation was exquisite beyond words; but it lasted only a few moments, and I awoke. As I was to learn later, my mental control had been overwhelmed by my emotions; so the tiresome body asserted its claim and pulled me back. And now I had a (to me) wonderful new idea: Was it possible to regain at will the glory of the dream? Could I *prolong* my dreams?'

The key to Fox's technique, observing incongruities in dreams and clearly recognizing them as such, sounds remarkably easy; but in practice it is one of the most difficult things to accomplish. Fox himself tried many times to tell himself that he was in fact dreaming, without any change taking place; but when he did manage to acquire the knowledge, the same thing happened. The process of recognizing incongruities and prolonging the dream into waking consciousness released the astral body and Fox was able to pass through seemingly solid walls and 'mould matter into new forms'.

He found, however, that the effort of prolonging the dream produced a pain in the region of the pineal gland, which he took to be a warning to return to the body. He also found that in the last moments of prolonging the dream he experienced a dual consciousness. He could feel himself standing in his dream as well as being in his bed and seeing the bedroom.

The next stage of his experimentation stemmed from the question, what would happen if he were to disregard the pain and force his dream consciousness even further?

Fox embarked upon this with some nervousness, finding when he did so that he experienced a 'click' in his brain followed by the sensation of being 'locked out' in his dream and completely disassociated from his physical body. In this stage, the sense of dual consciousness vanished and he considered himself to be occupying a new dimension, free of time as he had formerly known it. He had astrally projected.

It was only a brief experience, For with it came a feeling of utter loneliness followed by panic. He then felt the same cerebral 'click' and found himself back in his physical body, in a complete cataleptic trance (see p.50). He only regained control of the physical organism with the greatest of effort: 'I jumped out of bed with great joy, and immediately collapsed upon the floor, being overwhelmed with nausea. I felt ill for two or three days afterwards.'

It is as well to repeat at this point that astral projection can be dangerous and to give Fox's list of possible consequences:

1. Heart failure, or insanity, arising from shock.
2. Premature burial (arising from catalepsy).
3. Obsession.
4. Severance of the cord.
5. Repercussion effects upon the physical vehicle.

In Fox's experience, the body remains in a semi-rigid condition. Though the eyes are closed the surroundings are somehow plainly visible, as well as the atmosphere — Fox describes the experience as being like particles of dust illuminated by the sun. Behind this, on the edge of visibility, is what he curiously describes as a mass of frogs' eggs, blue-grey in colour and vibrating. There is also the consciousness of strange atmospheric stresses — something like an intense 'before the storm' feeling.

Up to this point, Fox had never achieved projection without a break in consciousness: there was always the feeling that something was holding him back. His solution was to force his incorporeal self through the doorway of the pineal gland so that it 'clicked' behind him:

It was done, when in the trance condition, simply by concentrating upon the pineal gland and willing to ascend through it. The sensation was as follows: my incorporeal self rushed to a point in the pineal gland and hurled itself against the imaginary trap-door ... If the impetus was insufficient to take me through, then the sensation became reversed; my incorporeal self subsided and became again coincident with my body, while the astral light died down to normal. Often two or three attempts were required before I could generate sufficient will-power to carry me through.

William Gerhardie

In 1934 William Gerhardie published what was ostensibly a novel called *Resurrection* containing what were, self-confessedly, genuine personal experiences. Like Oliver Fox, Gerhardie was able to exteriorize in his astral body by recognizing the fact that he was dreaming. He became conscious of the fact that the situation being enacted in his dream was ridiculous and this consciousness indicates a state between dreaming and waking — one in which the sleeping consciousness and the waking consciousness are more or less in coincidence with each other.

As soon as Gerhardie realized that he was dreaming he 'woke up'. He stretched out his hand to turn on the lamp above his bed, but found that he was grasping only empty space. It then became clear that he was, in fact, functioning outside his physical body. He felt himself being pushed out horizontally and placed on his feet.

> At the back of me was a coil of light like a luminous garden hose resembling the strong broad ray of dusty light at the back of a dark cinema projecting on the screen in front. To my utter astonishment the broad cable of light at the back of me illuminated the face on the pillows I recognized as my own, as if attached to the brow of the sleeper. It was myself, not dead, but breathing peacefully, my mouth slightly open ...

In his astral state he was unable to turn the door handle in the normal way but was quite capable of passing through apparently solid matter; he also caught a glimpse of himself in the bathroom mirror, dressed exactly as the body on the bed. He was able to move with an intense feeling of lightness but was unable to move the objects in the room. He became aware, once outside his flat, that the feeling of lightness increased the farther away he moved from the physical body; he was also aware that he had the ability to go wheresoever he chose. But, feeling cautious, he decided to return to his physical body and he thus describes his re-entry:

> My consciousness became dimmed. It seemed to be as if a dozen coolies, among much screeching and throbbing, were lowering with the utmost precaution under expert direction, from a noisy crane, which seemed to reverberate in my own brain, some precious burden which was myself into some vessel which presently became myself. Then with a jerk which shook me as though the machinery dropped into my bowels weighed a ton, I opened my eyes.

Experimental Projection

The experiments of the French investigator Hector Durville included astral projections induced when the subject was in deep 'magnetic' trance. They apparently confirmed the existence of the silver cord ('Usually this is cylindrical, but may sometimes appear to be a sort of ribbon') and, on the question of whether the astral body is clothed, Durville stated that the clothes of the projected phantoms seemed to be composed of a kind of fluidic gauze. Calcium sulphide screens were set up some distance from the subject and the suggestion given that the phantom should approach one of them. Whichever one was chosen by the phantom glowed with added brilliance. Durville's conclusions (as set out in his little-known book *Le Fantôme des Vivants*) were as follows:

1. Projection of the astral body is a certain fact, capable of being demonstrated by means of direct experiment. The conclusion is that conscious, or living force, is independent of matter and that individuality consists of a physical body, an intelligent soul, and a vital link between the two — the astral body.
2. Because this astral body, or phantom, can exist and function apart from the physical body, it must also be a strong argument for life after death: that is, immortality may be capable of scientific verification.

The Consequences of Habit

Habitual astral projection, though it might seem desirable to some people, has its disadvantages; indeed, it might be argued with some justice that conscious projection is against the natural order of things, for if it were an ability we were 'meant' to enjoy, we should all do it as a matter of course, like walking or seeing. The French astral projector

'Yram' wrote of the ease (which one can imagine to be extremely awkward, and even dangerous, at times) with which he was able to project after prolonged experimentation: 'It has happened at times that I have found myself projected, standing beside the body, at the same instant as I closed my eyes, and without experiencing any particular sensations ... The practice of projection becomes such a habit that there have been times when I have come back to my body in order to make sure that I was really projected and not sleep-walking. This will give some idea of the striking reality of this state.'

Incapacity

This is the term used by Sylvan Muldoon to describe the slowing-down of the physical processes so as to facilitate astral projection. It involves the slowing-down of the heartbeat and the pulse, and it should be obvious that *no one with any kind of heart or respiratory troubles should attempt this technique.*

You should lie and relax yourself as much as you can. The ability to lie perfectly still and listen to your body processes — above all to the regular pulsating beat of the heart — is not easy. It involves a high degree of concentration, but eventually you will acquire the knack of feeling the heart's pulsations in any part of your body. When this stage is reached, the next step is to reduce the speed of the pulsations, which is done by concentrating on the heart and directing it to slow down. *Slow* and *steady* pulsation of the heart facilitates projection, and bringing this about is an ancient method of exteriorizing the astral body. It hardly needs pointing out that the aim of this technique is to simulate the conditions during sleep, the period when most spontaneous astral projections occur.

Muldoon's technique for slowing down the normal life rhythms may be compared with Celia Green's more scientific suggestion that there is some reason to associate ecsomatic (out-of-the-body) experiences with decreased muscle tone. Some 33 per cent of her subjects reported that their experience had been accompanied by relaxation of the muscles — even in cases where stress was a powerful factor in pushing out the double. Relaxation and meditative techniques, as has long been known, are therefore conducive to the practice of conscious astral projection.

CHAPTER FOUR

SOME TESTIMONIES

A book many times the length of this one could be filled with the personal testimonies of those who have experienced astral projection, both voluntarily and involuntarily. In isolation, each might be criticized by the sceptic, and suitably 'logical' explanations might be given to explain away what otherwise puts an abiding question mark over scientific materialism. But in the mass, these personal accounts form an immense barrier to scepticism; their impressiveness is overwhelming, and anyone with an open mind must conclude that beneath them all lies a firm foundation of truth.

Though there are many common features, each astral journey is a unique experience; just as we all see the material world in different ways, so the features of the astral plane, and indeed the methods used and sensations experienced in reaching it, vary from traveller to traveller. To the novice, then, the testimonies of those who have gone before are of immense value, being a cumulative record of what a host of travellers have found beyond the body.

Case 1

A fairly typical case was narrated by Sylvan Muldoon in *The Occult Review* for January 1931. It concerned a Mrs B., an American lady who experienced many out-of-the-body journeys. Most of these had been involuntary projections, usually in the early hours of the morning and preceded by physical numbness.

Just before projection took place, Mrs B. would feel as though she was caught up in a powerful current; she would experience pain and 'snapping' in her head, which passed into a sensation of pleasing lightness. During projection she was unable to direct her astral body and had to remain content with sailing along wherever carried. She was usually in distress during projection (this would seem to be an untypical experience), with a painful tightness in the throat, which might become so unbearable as to force her to return to the physical body.

During the journey reported by Muldoon, Mrs B. found herself projected in her astral body to the parlour of a strange palatial house. Muldoon then quotes Mrs B.'s own words:

From the parlour I soared up a great stairway

and down a hall into a room where lay an old
lady. I approached the bed with some
hesitation, although I felt sure of being
invisible. Suddenly she awakened, and acted as
if she could see me, for she sat up on her
elbow and looked straight at me.

I was much embarrassed at being there in a
strange house like a thief. She no doubt thought
me a ghost of the dead ... I began to retreat,
going over instead of around the stair-railing,
and down — down — down, with an
accompanying sinking feeling at the pit of my
stomach. Then there was a 'zinging' in my ears,
and in a moment I was sitting up breathless in
my physical body in my own bed.

Apart from the precise details of the sensations Mrs
B. felt during astral projections, the postscript to her
journey is the most fascinating part of her
experience. Two years after this astral journey she
visited Concord, some forty miles from where she
lived in New Hampshire, to visit her cousin. This
cousin had recently bought a house, completely
furnished, from the estate of an elderly maiden lady,
a Miss M., who had died some time before.

Mrs B. had never been to her cousin's house
before:

A maid ushered me into the same parlour in
which I had stood that night when out of my
body. Looking around I knew I had seen the
place before, but could not quite remember,

until I stepped into the hall, when my cousin came down the stairs to welcome me. I had found the place of my astral adventure!

It transpired, of course, that the old lady, in whose bedroom Mrs B. had appeared two years before, was Miss M.[1]

Case 2

In the early years of psychical research, it became clear that the appearances of apparitions were not invariably associated with death or trauma. Wraiths or simulacrums were observed at a distance from the 'communicator's' body without there being any tragic circumstances attached to their appearance. It was enough, it seemed, that the individual's thoughts were concentrated sufficiently strongly on a distant object, person or place for a simulacrum to appear.

But was this phantom the result of telepathy, of the communicator's thoughts acting in some way on the mind of the percipient? Or was it, on the other hand, some part of the communicator that had somehow detached itself and become visible to the percipient? The first hypothesis is undoubtedly correct in some cases, but in general this violation of one mind by another does not fit the facts.

The alternative theory, as we have seen in this book, postulates the existence of an astral double which is projected, consciously or unconsciously, beyond the communicator's material body. In corroboration of this, there are the many testimonies in which people bring back vivid and entirely accurate memories of places they have never visited. The *reality* of such experiences needs to be stressed. Take, for instance, the following case recorded by F.W.H. Myers:

One night last January, 1872, I, Ann Amherst, dreamt that I saw Mary de Lys and that I had a large pin in my hand and in speaking to her energetically about something I gave her a tremendous prick on the forefinger of her right hand. She made a face as of one in pain which I saw distinctly in my dream and said: 'Oh, this pin! How it hurts! Why did you do it?' The next morning on coming downstairs I found her and Louey sitting together by the fire in the library. Mary was holding her finger, and with the same expression of pain I had seen in my dream, she said the same words, and I, feeling quite scared, thought for a moment I had done it and said to her and to Louey's astonishment: 'Did I do it?' She did not in the least know how or when it had been done and Louey had been looking in vain for a pin in Mary's dress that might have caused the prick. Before coming down in the morning and hearing what Mary said I had not mentioned my dream to a living soul. I should also state that both our bedroom doors were locked all night. The finger was bad for several days and had to be plastered up. It was the same finger and hand I had seen in my dream, the forefinger of the right hand.[2]

Case 3: Spontaneous Projection

As we have already seen, astral projection can be of two types — spontaneous and deliberate. In spontaneous projections, the person simply finds himself outside the body without knowing why or how the projection happened; often, however, there is a specific reason for this kind of projection, such as physical trauma. In conscious or deliberate projection, there is a specific and determined desire to project beyond the physical body, although success (it must be said) is not easy. Sometimes, through a number of factors, projection may be successful without the experimenter realizing the fact, and his phantom may be seen by others in a different locality though the projector remains unaware of his success.

A good example of spontaneous projection was given by Caroline D. Larsen in her book *My Travels in the Spirit World*:

Suddenly I underwent a very strange experience. A feeling of deep oppression and apprehension came over me, not unlike that which precedes a fainting-spell. I braced myself against it, but to no avail. The overpowering oppression deepened, and soon numbness crept over me until every muscle became paralyzed. In this condition I remained for some time. My mind, however, was still working as clearly as ever. At first I heard the music (downstairs) plainly, but soon the sounds began to slip away from me by degrees until finally everything became a blank, and I was unconscious to life and the world. How long this state lasted I do not know. What happened during this period I am also unable to relate. The next thing I knew was that I, myself, was standing on the floor beside my bed looking down attentively at my own physical body lying in it ... I recognized every line of that familiar face, pale and still as in death, the eyes tightly closed and the mouth partly open. The arms and hands rested limp and lifeless beside the body ... I turned and walked slowly towards the door, passed through it and into a hall that led to the bathroom ... Through force of habit I went through the motions of turning on the electric light, which, of course, I did not actually turn on. But there was no need for illumination, for from my body and face emanated a strong whitish light that lighted up the room brilliantly.'³

Case 4: Projection Under Anaesthetic

Equally typical of spontaneous projection, though it has some unusual features, this time as a result of anaesthetic, is the following, reported in the Theosophical magazine *Lucifer* in 1894:

I had a tooth out by gas on Monday, and while I was under the influence of the gas, I had the most extraordinary experience. After the first brief period of unconsciousness, I became aware that I was no longer on the physical plane; my body and all other physical objects seemed to have disappeared. In every direction stretched a dark blue vault, something like the sky on a summer night. I seemed to *have no form*, but round my formless self was a soft white light, which acted as a kind of formless body for me; and from it proceeded what I can only call a luminous 'wire', which I knew connected me with my physical body. Close to me, very nearly in contact, was another formless body of this soft white light, just like myself; and it shone with exactly the same intensity. At a considerable distance were other white lights, much less bright than myself and the one near me, stretching away as far as I could see.

For the time being I could really understand what it was to be formless and yet to retain individuality, and I said to myself: 'Of course formless beings can exist. How wonderful not to have understood it before. I remember it all.' But I knew that my ability to comprehend the formless state depended upon my being out of the body, and that when I returned to the body again I should, as before, be quite unable to understand such a state.

Then a voice began to speak. I cannot remember the exact words, but they were something like this: 'Know that formless beings do exist; and because you have obeyed the Law, and been clothed with a body which is material and dull and which gives great hindrance to things you can now comprehend, never again distrust the great teachings or incline to disbelief in states that are incomprehensible to you in your body.'

Then I felt impulses along the 'wire' connecting me with my body, and I knew I was returning to it. I seemed to descend in a spiral manner into my body; and the process of returning was most unpleasant. I did not *wish* to return, any more than people wish to die, as a rule. My first words when I woke up were, 'What a dreadful sensation!' and I was thinking of the return, not of the tooth, of which I had felt nothing.

Case 5: Dr Wiltse

Perhaps one of the most celebrated cases of spontaneous astral projection is that of Dr Wiltse. It first appeared in the *St Louis Medical and Surgical Journal* in November in 1899, but it was also reported in Volume VIII of the *Proceedings* of the Society for Psychical Research as well as in Myers's *Human Personality and the Survival of Bodily Death* (Volume II, pp.315-22). Here is Dr Wiltse's account of what he experienced as he was involuntarily projected from his physical body:

> With all the interest of a physician I beheld the wonders of my bodily anatomy, intimately interwoven with which, even tissue for tissue, was I, the living soul of that dead body ... I watched the interesting process of the separation of soul and body. By some power, apparently not my own, the Ego was rocked to and fro, laterally, as a cradle is rocked, by which process its connection with the tissues of the body was broken up. After a little time, the latter motion ceased, and along the soles of the feet, beginning at the toes, passing rapidly to the heels, I felt and heard, as it seemed, the snapping of innumerable small cords. When this was accomplished I began slowly to retreat from the feet, towards the head, as a rubber cord shortens ... As I emerged from the head I floated up and down and laterally like a soap-bubble attached to the bowl of a pipe until I at last broke loose from the body and fell lightly to the floor, where I slowly rose and expanded into the full stature of man. I seemed to be translucent, of a bluish cast and perfectly naked.

Dr Wiltse then directed his gaze to the bed and saw

his own 'dead' body lying just as he had taken pains to place it, partially on the right'side, the feet close together, and the hands clasped across the breast. Seeing it, he was surprised at the paleness of the face.

What Dr Wiltse's account emphasizes is that the process of astral projection is never precisely the same for everyone. One notes too the clarity of detail, such as the 'snapping of innumerable small cords'. Details like this tend to enforce the feeling that a real experience is being described and not just a vivid dream.

Case 6: The Reality of the Astral World

There are a number of cases in which people share dreams that are afterwards remembered in vivid detail. Such cases seem to reinforce the probability of an astral world interpenetrating our own to which, in sleep, the astral body can reach. The fact that two or more people can share the same astral experiences at the same time is explained by telepathy, now a well-established fact. Take the following remarkable case, related by Professor Hornell Hart. It concerns an American lawyer, Henry Armitt Brown:

> In the fall of 1865 ... while I was studying law in the city of New York, I retired to my room about midnight of a cold and blustering

evening. I remember distinctly hearing the clock strike twelve as ... drowsiness crept upon me and I slept. I had hardly lost consciousness when I seemed to hear loud and confused noises and felt a choking sensation at my throat, as if it were grasped by a strong hand. I awoke (as it seemed) and found myself lying on my back on the cobble-stones of a narrow street, writhing in the grip of a low-browed thick-set man with unkempt hair and grizzled beard, who with one hand at my throat and holding my wrists with the other threw his weight upon me and held me down ... Over and over we rolled upon the stones ... Presently I saw him reach forth his hand and grasp a bright hatchet ... I made one more tremendous fight for life, for a second I held my enemy powerless and saw with such a thrill of delight as I cannot forget the horror-stricken faces of friends within a rod of us rushing to my rescue. As the foremost of them sprang upon the back of my antagonist he wrenched his wrist away from me. I saw the hatchet flash above my head and felt instantly a dull blow on the forehead. I fell back on the ground, a numbness spread from my head over my body, a warm liquid flowed down upon my face and into my mouth, and I remember the taste as of blood.

Then I thought I was suspended in the air a few feet above my body, I could see myself as if in a glass, lying on the back, the hatchet

sticking in my head ... I heard the weeping of
friends, at first loud, then growing fainter ...
With a start, I awoke ... My watch told me I had
not been more than half an hour asleep.

Early the next morning I joined an intimate
friend with whom I spent much of my time
... Suddenly he interrupted me with the
remark that he had dreamed strangely of me
the night before ... 'I fell asleep,' he said,
'about twelve and immediately dreamed that
I was passing through a narrow street when
I heard noises and cries of murder. Hurrying
in the direction of the noise, I saw you lying
on your back, fighting a rough labouring
man, who held you down. I rushed forward,
but as I reached you he struck you on the
head with a hatchet and killed you instantly.
Many of our friends were there and we cried
bitterly ...'

'What sort of man was he?' I asked. 'A thick-set
man, in a flannel shirt and rough trousers; his
hair was uncombed and his beard was grizzly
and of a few days' growth.'

Within a week I was in Burlington, New Jersey.
I called at a friend's house. 'My husband,' said
his wife to me, 'had such a horrid dream about
you the other night. He dreamed that a man
killed you in a street fight. He ran to help you,
but before he reached the spot your enemy had
killed you with a great club.'

> 'Oh, no,' cried the husband across the room, 'he killed you with a hatchet...'[4]

Here the reality of the experience comes across dramatically. There seems no ascribable cause for the 'dream' (one wonders what part weather conditions might play in facilitating the passage into the astral world: this particular night was 'cold and blustering') or for the mechanisms that set up the telepathic links between these three friends. But we are justified, surely, in thinking that this kind of shared experience takes place, literally; in other words, that these events are actual, but in another plane. We notice the synchronicity — the 'murder' took place in Brown's dream at midnight, while his first friend fell asleep 'about twelve' and immediately plunged into this astral dream. But how or why such things happen is for the moment beyond conjecture.

Case 7: Miss Moberly and Miss Jourdain

Though not strictly a case of astral projection, the extraordinary experiences of C.A.E. Moberly, Principal of St Hugh's Hall, Oxford, and E.F. Jourdain, her Vice-President elect, are worth recounting to show how a dimension other than the one we normally inhabit can, at certain points, align itself with what we call the present.

The explanation seems to be that the two ladies

shared the memories of Marie Antoinette of the Petit Trianon at Versailles as the Queen, under great duress and discomfort, looked back at the place she loved so much while being held in the Manège in Paris on 10 August 1792 by the Legislative Assembly. The circumstances, as will be described later, were such as to bring about a species of astral projection, a vivid reconstruction of Marie Antoinette's last hours at the Trianon, that continues to reverberate through time.

On an August afternoon in 1901 Miss Moberly and Miss Jourdain, after some days of sight-seeing in Paris, decided to visit Versailles. They walked round the palace, with interest though not with undue enthusiasm, after which Miss Moberly suggested that they visit the Petit Trianon, the small 'farmhouse' where Marie Antoinette had amused herself. It had been hot all the week, but on that day the sky was a little overcast and there was a lively wind blowing.

Looking on their map they worked out the general direction to the Petit Trianon from the main palace and set off, both feeling vigorous. They passed the Grand Trianon and came upon a broad green drive, which was quite deserted. This in fact would have taken them to the Petit Trianon, but instead of following the drive they crossed it and went up a lane in front of them. Miss Moberly was surprised that her companion did not ask the way from a woman shaking a white cloth out of the window of a building at the corner of the lane, but she concluded that Miss Jourdain must know where she was going.

They continued on their way until they came upon a convergence of three paths. Not knowing which one to take they decided to ask the way from two men whom they saw on the central path. They afterwards called them gardeners, because they remembered a wheelbarrow near by and something that may have been a pointed spade; but they were really dignified officials, dressed in long greenish-coloured coats and small three-cornered hats. The men directed them straight on. A note in the 1924 edition of *An Adventure*, the book in which the experiences of Miss Moberley and Miss Jourdain were published, states that one man looked older than the other and that both were 'very grave'.

From this point an extraordinary depression came over Miss Moberly which steadily deepened. There seemed no reason for it, but the feeling became 'quite overpowering' when they reached the point where the path ended, to be crossed by another, right and left. In front of them was a garden kiosk, like a small bandstand, beside which a man was sitting: 'Everything suddenly looked unnatural, therefore unpleasant; even the trees behind the building seemed to have become flat and lifeless, *like a wood worked in tapestry*. There were no effects of light and shade, and no wind stirred the trees.'[5]

The man was wearing a cloak and a large shady hat. His face was described by Miss Moberly as 'most repulsive — its expression odious'. She asked Miss Jourdain which way they should go, though she thought to herself that nothing would induce her to go to the left.

At that moment they heard someone running up behind them. This turned out to be 'distinctly a gentleman'; he was 'tall, with large dark eyes, and had crisp curling black hair under the same large sombrero hat'. Miss Jourdain remembered that he had buckled shoes. He was greatly excited and called out, "'Mesdames, Mesdames" (or "Madame" pronounced more as the other), "il ne faut" (pronounced *fout*) "pas passer par là." He then waved his arm, and said with great animation, "par ici ... cherchez la maison."'

The man was determined that the ladies should turn to the right, which fell in with Miss Moberly's wishes. She looked away for a moment but when she turned to thank the man he had disappeared.

At last they reached the Petit Trianon. Below the terrace Miss Moberly saw a lady. She was sitting, holding out a paper as though to look at it at arm's length. She wore a shady white hat perched on a good deal of fair hair. Miss Moberly thought she was a tourist, though her dress seemed old-fashioned and 'rather unusual'. It should be noted that though they passed close by the lady, Miss Jourdain never saw her, although she remembered drawing her skirt away, 'with a feeling as though someone were near and I had to make room'. Miss Moberly, however, looked straight at the woman, but some 'indescribable feeling' made her turn away, annoyed at the woman's presence.

They then ascended to the terrace, Miss Moberly feeling as if they were walking in a dream — 'the stillness and oppressiveness were so unnatural'. They met one other person there, a young man with the jaunty manner of a footman, but with no livery, who suddenly stepped out on to the terrace, banging a door behind him, who showed them the way into the house.

Such were the main details of Miss Moberly's account. Both she and Miss Jourdain felt that the Petit Trianon was haunted and Miss Jourdain later admitted to a feeling of depression and anxiety at certain points on their walk.

Over the years that followed they began to piece together a possible explanation for their experience. On 10 August 1792 the Tuileries were sacked by the revolutionary mob. The royal family escaped early in the morning to the Hall of the Assembly, where they were penned up for many hours, within the sound of the mob and the massacre of their servants and guards. It seemed to Miss Moberly and Miss Jourdain that they had inadvertently entered within an act of the Queen's memory, which would explain the sensation of being completely shut in and oppressed: 'What more likely, they thought, than that during those hours in the Hall of the Assembly, or in the Conciergerie, she had gone back in such vivid memory to other Augusts spent at Trianon that some impress of it was imparted to the place?'[6]

Subsequent research filled in, to their satisfaction at least, the possible identities of the people they had met: the Comte de Vaudreuil, a Creole marked by smallpox, one of the Queen's innermost circle of friends who had played the enemy's part by persuading the King to allow the politically dangerous play of *Le Mariage de Figaro* to be acted, was the man by the kiosk. The running man was a messenger sent to the Trianon to warn the Queen of the approach of the Paris mob. The two 'gardeners' were the *garçons jardiniers de la Chambre* : on 5 October 1789 the guards were two of the three Bersy brothers, who, with one Breval, were usually on duty whenever the Queen was at Trianon. The lady on the terrace was, of course, Marie Antoinette herself.

The Moberly-Jourdain case, as Lucille Iremonger showed in her book *The Ghosts of Versailles*, is not as straightforward as the narratives in *An Adventure* would lead the reader to suppose. The Society of Psychical Research thought little of the case when it was first brought to their notice, and the whole question of the documentary evidence on which *An Adventure* is based is complex and, from an evidential point of view, unsatisfactory.

And yet no one has ever suggested that Miss Moberly and Miss Jourdain perpetrated a literary hoax; and though both ladies had inner histories that explain much that is puzzling about their adventure, there seems no question of their fundamental integrity. They clearly believed *something* happened to them at Versailles that was out of the ordinary. The sceptic will not find it difficult to demolish their claims; but given their integrity, what *might* have happened?

To those with a more open mind, and with other better documented cases of this type in mind, it is possible to see the Moberly-Jourdain case as an intrusion of the astral world into the consciousness of two sensitive Oxford spinsters.

The ladies themselves thought they had been caught up in an 'act of memory' by which Marie Antoinette, penned up on an intolerably hot afternoon, cast her mind back to the Petit Trianon and its grounds: 'If only she could fly to that beloved spot away from this horrible smell of blood, what happiness it would be to her jaded spirits!'[7]

We have already seen how desire is a potent factor in bringing about astral projection. It is conceivable that the astral world contains the impress of all events and that, in this dream of desire generated by her terrible situation, the Queen projected herself into the astral plane and relived her last moments at the Trianon. It is conceivable, too, that Miss Moberley and Miss Jourdain, both, in spite of their claims, extremely susceptible to psychic phenomena, formed an unconscious desire to experience the reality of Versailles and the Petit Trianon as it had been over a hundred years previously and that this somehow projected them into astral coincidence with Marie Antoinette's 'act of memory'.

Case 8: W.E. McBride

Sometimes concern or anxiety replaces or compounds desire as an impetus to astral projection. The need to be near a loved-one who is felt to be in danger or distress is often so powerful as to eject the astral body. The case of Walter E.

McBride is an example.

Just before Christmas 1935, Walter McBride, a bachelor farmer from Indian Springs, Indiana, began to feel concerned, for no apparent reason, for the health of his father, who lived some miles away. He went to bed at about eight o'clock and soon afterwards felt himself floating about the room in a whitish light that cast no shadows. He felt himself to be wide awake at the time and after moving upwards he turned vertical and clearly saw his physical body lying on the bed.

He continued to float upwards, through the solid matter of the building and then realized that he was moving northwards towards his father's home. He passed through the walls of his father's house and stood at the foot of his bed, in which his father was reclining. The father looked at the apparition of his son with some surprise but did not seem to hear when McBride spoke. McBride then realized that his father was well, whereupon he found himself travelling back again to his own bedroom. He once more saw his physical body lying on the bed where he had left it. After he had re-entered his body he was instantly alert and felt no drowsiness.

He then got up and wrote an account of his experience, dating it 23 December 1935. Two days later, on Christmas Day, he visited his father, who verified that he had seen an apparition of McBride standing at the foot of his bed. The father, too, had written an account of the incident and had also made a note of the time and date — both of which coincided.[8]

Single and Multiple Experiences

According to the surveys made by Celia Green at the Institute of Psychophysical Research at Oxford, the majority of people who claimed to have had an out-of-the-body experience only had it once. These Celia Green called 'single' cases and accounted for just over 60 per cent of her subjects. The number who had two, three, four or five experiences fell off sharply, but, curiously, the number who said they had had more than six experiences increased to over 20 per cent. The reason seems to be related to the ability to project at will, or at least the capability of exercising some control over projections when they happen spontaneously.

It is useful to bear in mind Celia Green's terminology: the out-of-the-body experience, or astral projection, is referred to by her as an 'ecsomatic' experience. Within this are two distinctions: a 'parasomatic' experience is one 'in which the percipient is associated with a seemingly spatial entity with which he feels himself to be in the same kind of relationship as, in the normal state, he is with his physical body'. An 'asomatic' experience is an ecsomatic state 'in which the subject is temporarily unaware of being associated with any body or spatial entity at all'.[9]

It is interesting to note that from Celia Green's researches, asomatic experiences are much more common than parasomatic ones.

The Youngest Astral Projector?

Out-of-the-body experiences can happen to anyone, no matter what age, though it is likely that in 'single' cases the experience will occur between the ages of about fifteen to thirty-five. Multiple experiences of projections, however, often occur in childhood, after which the ability is lost.

The earliest age at which an ecsomatic experience occurred is reported by Celia Green to have been at eighteen months. Another childhood case involved fairly basic reflections on the question of personal identity — that is, concentration on questions such as 'What am I?', or 'Who am I?' — to produce separation from the physical body.

Case 9: Transference of Sense Impressions

Sylvan Muldoon recounted an interesting experiment that showed how the astral body could 'feel'. Muldoon wished to find out whether his dog, Jack, could see his astral body. He allowed Jack to sleep in his room and then exteriorized. For a few nights Jack slept too soundly for Muldoon's astral presence to arouse him; but then one night the dog happened to awake when Muldoon exteriorized. Jack was standing and looking at Muldoon's physical body, waiting for an invitation, it seemed, to jump up on the bed.

The dog did not appear to see Muldoon's astral body, though Muldoon went through the motions of beckoning and calling him. Jack continued to watch the physical body, though once he lifted his head and sniffed in the direction of the phantom.

Finally, Jack jumped on to the bed and pushed himself up against Muldoon's physical body, and as he did so a strange thing happened: 'The physical was rocked upward and downward slightly from the action of the springs, as the dog's weight landed upon the bed, and the astral, in exactly the same time, rocked upward and downward in the air, in perfect harmony with the movement of the physical, although the astral body was in the vertical and the physical was in the horizontal position.'[10]

But even more strange was that as Jack curled up against the physical body it felt to Muldoon as if he were curling up against the side of his astral body and he continued to feel Jack's weight against him until he was physically active again. Muldoon's explanation was that the sense of touch is transmitted over a line of force into the astral body while it remains in what he calls 'cord-activity' range.

One could go on multiplying examples and bringing forward witnesses. Many out-of-the-body stories are on record from hundreds of ordinary people who have suddenly, for no apparent reason, found themselves beyond the body in a second vehicle of consciousness, while there is a similar abundance of documentation from people who have consciously and deliberately set about separating the astral double from the physical body.

The source material for a comprehensive study of the subject is, then, enormous and ever growing. The cumulative effect of the published testimonies is overwhelmingly in favour of a non-materialist, even non-psychological, theory to explain their occurrence. Only a hardened sceptic would state categorically that all these experiences were hallucinatory or the result of a diseased mind. It seems much more likely that the ancient teachings, which St Paul clearly acknowledged, were right: that there is within us all another body, a subtle vehicle in which our essential consciousness, the real 'I', dwells.

What this hypothesis means for the question of belief in an after life is even more momentous but beyond the scope of this book. I can find no better words with which to conclude than those of Professor Hornell Hart:

No matter how deeply convinced I, as the author of this book, may feel, after my search for the full evidence on both sides of the survival question, my own conclusions are not the really significant outcome. Quite sincerely, I am *not* primarily concerned with winning you over to my own personal decision. Far more important, as an ultimate product of this study, should be the stimulation of innumerable readers to weigh the evidence, to seek with all sincerity to free themselves from preliminary prejudices, and to reach their own conclusions in the light of the evidence. You are the jury.[11]

NOTES

Chapter One

1 John Davy, 'The Evidence for Life After Life', *Observer Magazine*, 8 April 1979.
2 Quoted by Davy, ibid.
3 J.G. Bennett, *Witness*, Turnstone Books (1974), pp.3-4.
4 ibid, p.261.
5 William Kingsland, *Rational Mysticism* (1924), p.323.
6 *J.S.P.R.*, Vol 50, No 779, March 1979, p.39.
7 Archie Matson, *The Waiting World*, Turnstone Books (1975), p.14.
8 Muldoon and Carrington, *The Projection of the Astral Body*, p.xv.
9 Crookall, *More Astral Projections*, p.xv.
10 Carrington, *Your Psychic Powers and How to Develop Them*, pp. 229-30.

11 Crookall, *More Astral Projections*, p.1.

12 ibid, p.xvi.

13 ibid.

14 Quoted by Crookall, *Techniques of Astral Projection*, p.66

15 G.N.M. Tyrrell, *Apparitions* (1943), p.78.

16 Celia Green, *Out-Of-The-Body Experiences*, p.41.

17 ibid, p.19.

Chapter Two

1 Hart, *The Enigma of Survival*, p.207.

2 Quoted by Ralph Shirley, *The Mystery of the Human Double*, p.10.

3 E.A. Wallis Budge, *From Fetish to God in Ancient Egypt*, Oxford (1934), XIV.

4 Catherine Crowe, *The Night-Side of Nature* (1848), VIII.

Chapter Three

1 Walker, *Beyond the Body*, p.101.

2 Maitland, *Life of Anna Kingsford*, Vol 1, p.240.

3 Crookall, *Techniques of Astral Projection*, p.47.

4 Grant, *The Magical Revival*, p.93.

5 Quoted by Crookall, *Techniques of Astral Projection*, p.29.

6 Muldoon and Carrington, *The Projection of the Astral Body*, p.167.

Chapter Four

1 *Occult Review*, January 1931, pp.31-2.
2 Quoted by Shirley, *The Mystery of the Human Double*, p.20.
3 Muldoon and Carrington, *The Projection of the Astral Body*, p.xxxvi.
4 Hart, *The Enigma of Survival*, pp.237-8.
5 C.A.E. Moberly and E.F. Jourdain, *An Adventure*, Faber (1955), p.33.
6 ibid, p.44.
7 ibid, pp.107-8.
8 Hart, *The Enigma of Survival*, pp.159-60.
9 Celia Green, *Out-of-The-Body Experiences*, p.17.
10 Muldoon and Carrington, *The Projection of the Astral Body*, p.57.
11 Hart, *The Enigma of Survival*, p.263.

BIBLIOGRAPHY

Barratt, William. *Deathbed Visions*, Methuen (1926). Reissued by Aquarian Press (1986).

Battersby, H.P. *Man Outside Himself*, Rider (n.d.).

Besant, Annie. *Man and His Bodies*, Theosophical Publishing House (1911).

Brennan, J.H. *Astral Doorways*, Aquarian Press (1971; 2nd edition 1986).

Broad, C.D. *Religion, Philosophy and Psychical Research*, RKP (1953).

Budge, E.A. Wallis. *The Egyptian Book of the Dead*, RKP (1950).

Carrington, Hereward. *Higher Psychical Development*, Aquarian Press (1978).

—. *Your Psychic Powers and How to Develop Them*, Aquarian Press (1976).

Crespigny, P.C. de. *This World — And Beyond*, Cassell (1934).

Crookall, Robert. *The Study and Practice of Astral Projection*, Aquarian Press (1961).

—. *The Techniques of Astral Projection*, Aquarian Press (1964).

—. *More Astral Projections*, Aquarian Press (1964).

—. *Psychic Breathing*, Aquarian Press (1979).

Cummins, Geraldine. *Travellers in Eternity*, Psychic Press (1948).

Eastman, M. 'Out-of-the-body experiences', *Proceedings of the Society for Psychical Research*, 53, pp.287-309.

Fodor, Nandor. *Encyclopedia of Psychic Science*, University Books (1966).

Fox, Oliver. *Astral Projection*, University Books (1962).

Garrett, Eileen J. *Adventures in the Supernormal* (1949).

Gerhardie, William. *Resurrection*, Cassell (1934).

Green, Celia. *Lucid Dreams*, Hamish Hamilton (1968).

—. *Out-of-the-Body Experiences*, Hamish Hamilton (1968).

—. *Apparitions*, Hamish Hamilton (1975) (with Charles McCreery).

Gurney, Edmund; Myers, F.W.H.; and Podmore, Frank. *Phantasms of the Living* (1887).

Hart, Hornell. *The Enigma of Survival: The Case For and Against an After Life*, Rider (1959).

Hill, Arthur J. *Man is a Spirit*, Cassell (1918).

Kilner, Walter J. *The Human Atmosphere*, Dutton (1911).

King, Francis. *Astral Projection, Magic and Alchemy*, Spearman (1971).

Larsen, Caroline. *My Travels in the Spirit World* (1927).

Leadbeater, C.W. *Man Visible and Invisible*, Theosophical Publishing House (1957).

—. *The Astral Plane: Its Scenery, Inhabitants and Phenomena*, Theosophical Publishing House (rep. 1968)

Leonard, Gladys. *My Life in Two Worlds*, Cassell (1931).

Lodge, Oliver. *The Survival of Man* (1919).

Maitland, Edward. *Life of Anna Kingsford* (2 vols), Redway (1896).

Mead, G.R.S. *The Doctrine of the Subtle Body in Western Tradition*, Stuart and Watkins (1967).

Monroe, Robert. *Journeys Out of the Body*, Souvenir Press (1972).

Muldoon, Sylvan J. *The Case for Astral Projection* (1936).

—. *The Projection of the Astral Body*, Rider (1958) (with Hereward Carrington).

Myers, F.W.H. *Human Personality and Its Survival of Bodily Death* (1902).

Ophiel. *The Art and Practice of Astral Projection*, Samuel Weiser (1961).

Oxenham, John. *Out of the Body*, Longmans Green (1941).

Powell, A.E. *The Astral Body and Other Astral Phenomena*, Theosophical Publishing House (1927).

Shirley, Ralph. *The Mystery of the Human Double*, Rider (1972).

Smith, Susy. *The Enigma of Out of the Body Travel*, Helix Press (1965).

Swedenborg, Emanuel. *The Spiritual Diary*, ed. G. Bush and J.H. Smithson (1883-1902).

Tymms, Ralph. *Doubles in Literary Psychology*, Bowes and Bowes (1949).
Walker, Benjamin. *Beyond the Body*, RKP (1974).
'Yram', *Practical Astral Projection*, Rider (n.d.).

INDEX
